Plymouth Colony:
The Pilgrims Settle
in New England

Mitchell Lane
PUBLISHERS

P.O. Box 196 • Hockessin, Delaware 19707

Titles in the Series

Plymouth Colony:
The Pilgrims Settle
in New England

Kathleen Tracy

Printing   1   2   3   4   5   6   7   8   9

Library of Congress Cataloging-in-Publication Data
Tracy, Kathleen.
       Plymouth Colony: the Pilgrims settle in New England/by Kathleen Tracy.
          p. cm.—(Building America.)
       Includes bibliographical references and index.
       ISBN 1-58415-459-4 (library bound)
       1. Pilgrims (New Plymouth Colony)—Juvenile literature. 2. Puritans—
Massachusetts—History—17th century—Juvenile literature. 3. Massachusetts—
History—New Plymouth—1620-1691—Juvenile literature. I. Title. II. Building America
(Hockessin, Del.)
F68.T75 2007
974.4'02—dc22
                                    2006006098
ISBN-10:1-58415-459-4   ISBN-13: 9781584154594

ABOUT THE AUTHOR: Kathleen Tracy has been a journalist for over twenty years. Her writing has been featured in magazines including *The Toronto Star*'s "Star Week," *A&E Biography* magazine, *KidScreen,* and *Variety.* She is also the author of numerous books for young readers, including *The Watergate Scandal* and *The Life and Times of Nathan Hale.*

PHOTO CREDITS: Cover, pp. 1, 3—Library of Congress; p. 6—North Wind Picture Archives; p. 9—National Portrait Gallery; p. 14—Corbis; p. 19—Library of Congress; p. 22—Andrea Pickens; p. 28—North Wind Picture Archives; p. 31—Library of Congress; pp. 34, 36—North Wind Picture Archives; p. 38—Library of Congress; p. 40—National Portrait Gallery

PUBLISHER'S NOTE: This story is based on the author's extensive research, which she believes to be accurate. Documentation of such research is contained on page 46.
      The internet sites referenced herein were active as of the publication date. Due to the fleeting nature of some web sites, we cannot guarantee they will all be active when you are reading this book.

PLB

Contents

*For Your Information

In 1587 a group of British colonists was dropped off at Roanoke. Three years later, in 1590, when a ship filled with provisions arrived, the settlement was deserted. The only clue to the colonists' fate was the word Croatoan—the name of a local Indian tribe—carved into a wooden post.

Chapter

The Lost Colony

As soon as John White stepped on dry land, he knew something was terribly wrong. It was far too quiet—chillingly quiet. The former artist was now governor of England's first colony in the Americas on Roanoke Island. He had been away for three years, delayed by weather and war and politics, and had finally returned with a boatload of provisions for his settlers . . . but the settlers were nowhere to be found.

He walked through the abandoned settlement, now covered with dust and in disrepair from disuse. There was no apparent sign of a struggle—no musket balls, nothing broken, no sign of bloodshed. There was just . . . nothing—except for the word *Croatoan* carved into a wooden post of the fort and the letters *CRO* carved into the trunk of a tree.

Those two cryptic clues were the last contact ever made with the Roanoke settlers. They had disappeared, never to be found. It was a shocking end to what had begun as a great adventure. While the settlement of Jamestown would eventually become famous as the first permanent English settlement in the New World, the Lost Colony of Roanoke would be America's first great unsolved mystery.

Establishing a permanent settlement in the Americas was the brainchild of flamboyant Englishman Sir Walter Raleigh, who had secured a charter from the queen that gave him ten years to colonize; otherwise the rights would revert to the Crown. Raleigh was much less concerned about exploration than he was about money. He envisioned a settlement being a home base from which he could organize raids on Spanish ships to steal their New World treasures.

In 1584, Raleigh sent an advance scout team led by Philip Amadas and Arthur Barlowe to look for an appropriate location. They chose the Outer Banks—a group of barrier islands off the coast of what is now North Carolina. They claimed the land in the name of Queen Elizabeth I and spent six weeks exploring the area and trading with the local native peoples.

In his journal, Barlowe seemed enraptured by the land, calling it "the most plentiful, sweet, wholesome and fruitful of all the world." He also noted that the Native Americans were "gentle, loving and faithful, void of all guile and treason."[1]

When they returned to England, they brought a surprise for Raleigh and the queen—two Algonquin Indians, Manteo and Wanchese. In a typical display of gallantry, Raleigh asked to name the land claimed by the captains Virginia in honor of Elizabeth, who was also known as the Virgin Queen.

In the spring of 1585, Sir Richard Grenville was commissioned by Raleigh to lead a fleet of seven ships to the New World. The venture did not get off to a promising start. First, when they arrived at the Outer Banks, the lead ship hit a sandbank and the resulting flooding ruined most of the expedition's food. Then Grenville discovered a silver cup was missing after visiting with some local Indians. His response was to burn the tribe's chief to death.

Determined to carry out his orders, Grenville left behind 100 men as the first colonists, most of them former soldiers, who settled at the northern end of Roanoke Island. He appointed Ralph Lane

In 1585, Sir Richard Grenville led a fleet of ships to the New World. His mission was to establish a new settlement. Grenville left one hundred men at Roanoke Island, but this first attempt at colonization ultimately failed because of hostilities between the settlers and the native people there.

commander and left with a promise to return the following spring with provisions and additional colonists. But Grenville got side-tracked, attacking and plundering Spanish ships, and didn't make it back on time.

When Raleigh showed up in June, he found the settlement in a state of chaos. They had been unable to grow enough food, and when the local peoples declined to keep trading for it, the colonists became violent and kidnapped the son of the weroance, or leader, and used him as ransom.

Tired of such hardball tactics, the native peoples attacked an expedition Lane was leading down the Roanoke River. In retaliation, Lane killed the weroance, which would have surely escalated into more violence, so nobody was more relieved when Raleigh showed up than Lane. Not surprisingly, when Raleigh boarded his ship to return to England, Lane and all his men went with him.

In his written report of the ten months they had spent on the island, Lane said, "From whence the general in the name of the Almighty, weighing his anchors (having bestowed us among his fleet) for the relief of whom he had in that storm sustained more peril of wreck than in all his former most honorable actions against the Spaniards, with praises unto God for all, set sail the nineteenth of June 1586, and arrived in Portsmouth the seven and twentieth of July the same year."[2]

Not wanting to abandon the settlement, Grenville left behind fifteen of his men. He promised that more colonists would soon be on their way.

In 1587, a second group of colonists braved the three-month journey and arrived on the island July 22, 1587. There were 90 men, 17 women, and 9 children, all under the governorship of John White, an artist who had participated in the first voyage. His water-color drawings of the Roanoke voyages and the inland explorations would prove invaluable to later historians.

The plan was to pick up the fifteen men who had been left behind on the island, then continue up to the Chesapeake Bay. But when they got to Roanoke, the navigator surprised White by refusing to go any farther north, claiming unless he left immediately, he would be traveling back to London during the treacherous Atlantic storm season. Putting the safety of his ships and crew first, he insisted the colonists stay in Roanoke.

It was an unnerving welcome when there was no sign of the fifteen men—just the skeletal remains of one man—and they found the village a burned-out ruin. With the fate of the missing men looming over their heads, the colonists agreed to stay and rebuild. It's unclear whether they fully understood the situation they were walking into at first. Other than the Croatans on nearby Hatteras Island, most of the other local tribes now harbored ill will toward Europeans, based on their experiences with Lane and his men. However, they were determined to make it work. In this atmosphere of uncertainty, White's daughter gave birth to the first English child in the Americas on August 18. She was named Virginia Dare.

Governor White tried to reconcile with the native tribes that had been at odds with Lane, but they refused to reestablish friendly relations. That point was emphasized when colonist George Howe was killed while hunting for crabs.

The murder frightened the other colonists, who begged White to ask Queen Elizabeth to send more men to help protect the settlement. He agreed and immediately set sail for England, leaving behind several small boats for the settlers to use. Proving the navigator's point, White's ship was nearly destroyed during a ferocious storm, but he finally made it safely back.

He couldn't find a captain who would sail during the winter. By the time the storm season had passed, the queen had other more pressing matters on her mind; specifically, being attacked by Spain. To confront the impressive Spanish Armada, Elizabeth needed every available seaworthy ship—meaning the colonists would simply have to wait for reinforcements.

Worried for their safety, including that of his daughter and granddaughter, White managed to find two small ships that hadn't been called into service and set out for Roanoke in the spring of 1588. Being undersized, they were easy targets for pirates, who captured both ships and stole their entire cargo. With no provisions left, the ships returned to England.

It would be two more years before White was finally able to make his way back to Roanoke. He landed on the island on Virginia's third birthday, but there was no sign of life. He quickly organized a search team, but his men found nothing—no bones, no clothes, no indication they had ever been there.

Hoping that *Croatoan* had been a message, White thought the colonists had moved to Croatoan Island. Before he could send over a search team, a hurricane crashed into the Outer Banks and blew his fleet out to sea. Running low on provisions and having been pushed midway into the Atlantic by the power of the storm, White reluctantly returned to England, leaving behind any chance of finding out the colonists' fate.

Although nobody could have known at the time, it has since been determined that the colonists had arrived during the worst drought to hit the region in 400 years. Of the many theories offered in the centuries since the colony disappeared, one of the more intriguing is that to survive, the settlers were absorbed into the local indigenous population.

The Lumbee, who still reside in North Carolina, believe they are descendants of the tribe of Croatoans that assimilated the lost settlers. There is anecdotal evidence to support the claim. One is that the Lumbee are not recognized as a sovereign Indian nation, and as a result have no reservation, because they are too racially mixed. Fifty years after White's return in 1590, many of the Croatoans were said to be practicing Christianity and had taken the last names of Roanoke settlers.

It would be another seventeen years before England would again attempt to establish a colony in America. The success of Jamestown would inspire and lure other Europeans to the wild, dangerous New World that was also full of promise. Some came for adventure. Some came for profit. But the group that would most profoundly influence what would become American culture came for the most basic reason—for freedom.

Sir Walter Raleigh

Sir Walter Raleigh was either a charming entrepreneur or a clever con man. He was born into a well-regarded family and showed an adventuresome spirit from an early age. Given the choice of pursuing a career as a lawyer, minister, or soldier, Raleigh opted for the military—in large part because of the opportunities for piracy it offered.

Sir Walter Raleigh

While still a teenager, he volunteered to join the English force in France that was allied with the Protestant Huguenots, whom the Catholic French government was trying to exterminate. After leading troops against an Irish rebellion in 1580, Raleigh returned to London and managed to ingratiate himself to the queen, Elizabeth I. Elizabeth named him captain of the Queen's Guard, knighted him, and gave him land.

Although his attempt to found a colony on Roanoke Island failed, Raleigh brought back potatoes and tobacco from his expedition and is credited for popularizing smoking.

He eventually fell out of favor with the queen after she discovered he had secretly married one of her attendants, Elizabeth "Bessy" Throckmorton. Queen Elizabeth was outraged—and probably jealous of Bessy—and imprisoned Raleigh for a time in the Tower of London. He was then banished from the court.

For as popular as he had once been with the queen, he was intensely disliked and mistrusted by her successor, James I. In a sham of a trial, Raleigh was convicted in 1603 of conspiring to have James I removed and replaced by his cousin Arabella Stuart, who many believed had the more rightful claim to the throne. Raleigh's death sentence was commuted and he was instead again imprisoned in the Tower.

He was released in 1618 to lead an expedition in search of gold in Guyana, which ended in failure. When it was discovered Raleigh had attacked a Spanish settlement, the Spanish Ambassador to London demanded his execution. James I reinstated his sentence from fifteen years earlier.

Legend has it that before he was beheaded, Raleigh asked for, and was given, a final smoke of tobacco—thus beginning the tradition of giving a condemned prisoner a last cigarette before his execution.

FYI For Your Information

Martin Luther was a German monk who started the Protestant Reformation. Disillusioned with the Catholic Church and their practice of selling "indulgences" which would supposedly guarantee going to heaven, he protested. Luther believed the only way to gain salvation was through faith and unconditional belief in the gospels.

Chapter

Persecution

From the time that Constantine the Great made Catholicism the official religion of the Roman Empire up until the early sixteenth century, the Roman Catholic Church and the Pope wielded vast power in every European country. Over the centuries, the church had amassed a fortune in land holdings and cash—much of it through papal indulgences, payments to the clergy to help buy salvation. Such blatant greed and the Church's highly politicized activities left many Catholics angry and disillusioned.

In 1517 an Augustinian monk in Germany named Martin Luther protested by nailing up a list of 95 theses, expressing the view that salvation required only faith, and that no amount of good works or cash payments would make a difference. Thanks to the invention of the printing press, Luther's theses were distributed far and wide, generating a lot of support. The Protestant Reformation had begun.

While the battle of religious philosophies raged on the continent, England remained mostly an uninvolved observer—until Henry VIII needed a way to get a divorce from Catherine of Aragon, the daughter of Ferdinand and Isabella of Spain.

Although Catherine had been pregnant seven times, she and Henry had only one living child—a girl named Mary. The others had either died after birth, were stillborn, or Catherine miscarried.

Henry had fallen in love with one of his mistresses, Anne Boleyn, and since at forty-two Catherine couldn't conceive anymore, Henry wanted to divorce her and start a family with Boleyn. According to Church law, divorce was not allowed. He petitioned the Pope to annul the marriage. Catherine—intent on protecting her daughter's right to the throne—countered by appealing directly to the Pope. The dispute went on for six years, until Anne Boleyn got pregnant.

Henry solved his problem by renouncing the authority of the Pope and proclaiming himself the head of the Church of England. Besides being free to get a divorce, Henry was now free to confiscate all Church land, worth a considerable fortune. Although Henry wasn't ever a true Reformist—just an opportunist—by the time of his death, a radical reformist movement had sprung up that was able to push their agenda through during Edward VI's reign.

Edward died after just six years on the throne, and his very Catholic half sister, Mary, became Queen. Suddenly Protestants found themselves out of favor and persecuted. The winds shifted again when Elizabeth I took the throne in 1558. While she didn't accept papal authority—which meant, for example, that Anglican priests were now allowed to be married—the ceremonies and adherence to scripture remained much the same. Elizabeth had no interest in letting any fringe groups mold the church in their image.

The Puritans were such an extremist group. They believed the Anglican Church should be "purified" of all Roman Catholic practices and were constantly clashing with bishops over it. When Elizabeth died in 1603, James I was determined to deal with such disobedience harshly. James was an equal-opportunity persecutor—he went after Catholics and Protestant extremists with equal fervor.

Fearing for their lives, Puritan Separatists from the town of Scrooby decided to leave England for Holland, known for its religious tolerance. They settled first in Amsterdam and later Leyden. Although they were free to worship as they pleased, because they were foreigners, the Puritans—most of whom had been successful craftsmen in England—were not allowed to join any of the Dutch guilds. Forced to take low-paying jobs, they struggled financially. The biggest concern for the Puritans was the worry that Holland's permissiveness was a bad influence on their children, who had started rebelling against their parents' strict rules.

What the Puritans wanted was a place where they could dictate both the religious and social order without outside interference. There was only one place where they could literally start such a community—across the sea in untamed Virginia. Jamestown had been successfully settled beginning in 1607 through the Virginia Company of London. A rival group of investors calling themselves the Virginia Company of Plymouth was eager to establish their own colony to recoup losses from earlier failed efforts. This second group granted the Puritans a patent to colonize on their land in Virginia.

The Separatists who agreed to go pooled their money and bought a ship, the *Speedwell,* for the voyage. They also chartered, or rented, a second ship called the *Mayflower,* whose captain was Christopher Jones. They boarded the *Speedwell* in Leyden, and after meeting up with the *Mayflower,* sailed to Plymouth in the southern English county of Devon. Once the ships were loaded with provisions, they set sail on August 5, 1620—only to have the *Speedwell* start leaking, forcing both ships to return to port, where the *Speedwell* was repaired.

They set sail again on August 21, but 300 miles out to sea, the *Speedwell* sprang another leak. For a second time, they were forced to run back. At this point, several frustrated Puritans changed their minds and returned to Leyden. Rather than waste any more time on the *Speedwell,* the rest decided to all cram together on the *Mayflower* and leave the other ship in Plymouth.

On September 20, they left England for the last time. The Puritans had been already living on the ships for nearly six weeks—almost as long as the sixty-six-day trip across the Atlantic would take.

The *Mayflower* made good time for the first month in the late summer weather. Of the 102 passengers who embarked, most were Puritans, but they had also welcomed others to join them to help defray the enormous cost of the voyage. Most of the Separatists were farmers by trade, but there were also craftsmen such as painters and carpenters. Myles Standish was a professional soldier who had been hired by the Puritans as a military adviser to deal with local natives. Several families brought their servants. Two hunting dogs, a mastiff and an English spaniel, also made the journey. There was a doctor on board, Sam Fuller, who came in handy when Elizabeth Hopkins gave birth to a son, whom she and her husband Stephen named Oceanus, and who brought the number of passengers to 103.

In the early weeks, the seas were calm enough that on occasion some of the more adventurous travelers would brave being on deck for some fresh air. Most of the time they stayed in their living quarters on the gun deck, which was only about five and a half feet high.

According to *Mayflower* historian Caleb Johnson, "The length of the deck from stem to stern was about 80 feet, of which about 12 feet at the back belonged to the gun room and was probably off-limits to the passengers. The width at the widest part was about 24 feet. Various hatches provided access to the cargo hold below. . . . Many of the families built themselves small little 'cabins,' simple wooden dividers nailed together, to provide a small amount of privacy. Others, especially the young single men, just took up any old spot."[1]

During the voyage, they ate dry biscuits and salted beef. Weather permitting, they would catch fish. If they wanted to cook, they would put charcoal in metal boxes, but in rough weather the risk of starting a fire was too great so most of their meals were cold and uncooked. Their beverage of choice was beer—which even the children drank—because they believed the water would make them ill.

The first month the *Mayflower* made good time, but starting in October they ran into frightening storms that tossed the boat violently, leaving most of the passengers horribly seasick. The torrents of rain leaked into the ship, leaving everyone chronically damp and chilled. The more nervous of the group fretted over whether the *Mayflower* was sturdy enough to complete the voyage, but Captain Jones assured everyone his ship was holding up just fine, leaks notwithstanding.

The cold, wet conditions took a physical toll. That, combined with a lack of drinking water and dwindling food supplies, left many of the passengers weak and sick. Dr. Fuller's servant, William Butten, fell ill and died on November 6. Three days later they sighted land for the first time.

The Puritans had intended to settle in northern part of Virginia near the Hudson River, where Manhattan is located today. The storms had blown them slightly off course, and the first land they saw was Cape Cod. When Jones turned the *Mayflower* south toward the Hudson River, he encountered vicious seas and nearly lost the ship. Tired, hungry, and eager to get on dry land, the Puritans decided to stay at Cape Cod.

The Puritans were Protestants who believed the Church of England contained too many elements of Catholicism. Persecuted by Queen Elizabeth I as extremists, the Puritans sought refuge in Holland, then came to the New World to establish a colony where they could freely worship their faith. They named their settlement New Plymouth.

Aware they had no legal right to settle in the area, on November 11, the Puritan leaders drafted and ratified the Mayflower Compact, a document establishing their self-ruling government. John Carver was named governor.

On November 21, they finally dropped anchor. Myles Standish led a small scouting party and determined there wasn't enough fresh water in the area. After several weeks of exploration, it was decided to settle on the western shore of Cape Cod Bay, which Edward Winslow described as "on a high ground, where there is a great deal of land cleared, and hath been planted with corn three or four years ago, and there is a very sweet brook runs under the hillside, and many delicate springs of as good water as can be drunk, . . . and in this brook much good fish in their seasons; on the further side of the river also much corn-ground cleared. . . . Our greatest labor will be fetching of our wood, which is half a quarter of an English mile. . . . What people inhabit here we yet know not, for as yet we have seen none."[2]

They named their settlement New Plymouth, and on December 21, 1620, disembarked to start their new life.

The excitement of finally having a home was tempered by the enormity of the work that lay ahead of them. There were no stores to buy food or clothes or beer or furniture. They would have to sew, build, or trade for what they needed. They would have to be completely self-sufficient and self-reliant. The settlers would also have to rely on one another.

For a group of devout people who had traveled so far for religious freedom, their faith was about to be sorely tested.

Sewing

It's hard for anyone today to comprehend just how difficult daily life was for a seventeenth-century colonist. Not only did they have to grow and harvest their own crops and hunt game or slaughter livestock, in the early years at Plymouth Colony they also had to make nearly everything they owned by hand, including clothes.

A woman spinning

Even back in England, unless they were rich, women were usually responsible for keeping the family clothed. In his book *Five Hundred Points of Good Husbandrie*, written in 1604, author Thomas Tusser observed, "Though Ladies may rend and buy new every day, good housewives must mend and buy new as they may."[3]

Fabric such as wool was brought over with other supplies from England or bought from traders who would pass through. In later years, sheep for wool, and spinning wheels and looms, would be imported so that women could make their own fabric.

The needles used by the Plymouth women were primitive compared to those used today. Humans have been sewing since the ice age, using needles made of bone. Starting in the Middle Ages, needles were made from small strips of bronze wire. One end of the wire was flattened on an anvil, then a hole was punched in it for the eye. The other end was filed to a point. There were so many needle makers in London that they formed their own guild.

Pins, which were used to attach certain pieces of clothing such as collars, were made in the same way, except instead of an eye, one end had a small loop of wire to make the head.

Depending on the materials available, clothes were fastened with either buttons or hooks. What the Puritans did *not* have were the big metal belt buckles usually depicted in pictures. Those did not come into fashion until much later and were erroneously added by eighteenth-century artists.

After the successful settlement of Plymouth, several other colonies were soon established, including Massachusetts, Virginia, Rhode Island, New Hampshire, and Connecticut. Many settlers, like the Puritans, came in search of religious freedom. Others came hoping to make their fortunes or simply for adventure. With the help of the American Indians, the colonists learned how to grow corn, and agriculture became an important industry.

Chapter

3

A Deadly Winter

The Puritans established their first settlement in an abandoned Indian village, whose residents had been decimated by an epidemic, probably smallpox. The women were to stay on the *Mayflower* while the men came ashore every day to build the necessary living quarters and storehouses. The only days they didn't work were on the Sabbath and when the winter weather turned too harsh. The Puritans didn't even take Christmas off, although William Bradford scolded several colonists who accepted Captain Jones' offer to have a few beers that day.

After clearing the hill, the colonists planned where each family's living quarters would be and marked off a 20-foot-by-20-foot space for the storehouse. They spent weeks gathering plant stalks, or thatch, to make enough roofs. They worked long hours, continually slowed by the weather. They finished the storage unit first, in late January, then started on the homes.

The brutal winter took a devastating toll on the colony. Of the twenty-nine women who had made the voyage, all but five would die that first winter. The first to die was Dorothy Bradford, who drowned after falling off the *Mayflower* into the frigid Atlantic. The others, including Rose Standish, Elizabeth Winslow, Sarah Eaton, and Mary Allerton, died of illness, such as scurvy, or exposure.

Many children were left orphaned. Priscilla Mullins, at sixteen the oldest of the colony's girls, was the only member of her family to survive the first year. Fourteen-year-old Elizabeth Tilley not only lost both parents but her aunt and uncle as well. The young Allerton girls, ages five and seven, lost their mother. Mary Chilton's father died in early December, and her mother died a month later. Only the Hopkins family survived the winter intact.

It is somewhat ironic that while Puritan men considered young girls weak, the girls proved to be the most resilient. Only two girls died, an 18 percent mortality rate, compared to 11 boys, a 36 percent death rate. Half the adult men died, and the women had a staggering 82 percent mortality rate. Captain Jones' crew also suffered, with half his men dying between December and April.

Some speculate the women were more prone to contract a virus because they were stuck inside the ship all those months, in the same way people today catch more colds in the winter—not because of the cold but because people are indoors more, exposing one another to more germs. Even though the weather was miserable, at least the men were getting fresh air and exercise, with easy access to fresh drinking water. Plus, when the men got sick, the women would take care of them, increasing their chance of catching a disease. Back then, people didn't know that illnesses were caused by microorganisms that could be avoided by washing hands, covering one's mouth while coughing, and other simple hygiene practices.

There was a lot of lingering sadness when the last of colonists were finally able to live full-time on land. For some of the women and children, they had been on board for eight months—since leaving Holland the previous July.

The *Mayflower* finally set sail for England in April, arriving in May. Neither Captain Jones nor the *Mayflower* would ever make it back to Plymouth. After returning to London, Jones took the ship on trade runs to France. He died the following spring, in March 1622.

There's no documentation on the ship until two years later. On May 26, 1624, the captain's widow and two other co-owners requested an appraisal, declaring the ship to be in ruins. The last recorded reference was the appraisal. It is assumed by most historians that the *Mayflower* was broken down for scrap wood.

Shortly after the *Mayflower* left Plymouth, Governor Carver suffered sunstroke and died. His wife, Katherine, died a month later, reportedly of a broken heart. William Bradford was selected to be the new governor of the dwindling community.

For all the death and loss, there were also hopeful beginnings. The colony's first marriage occurred May 12, 1621, between Edward Winslow and Susanna White. The most famous coupling would be the courtship and ultimate marriage between Priscilla Mullins and John Alden, who were immortalized by Henry Wadsworth Longfellow in his epic poem *The Courtship of Myles Standish*.

Standish's wife, Rose, died within a few months of landing in the New World. Lonely, Myles decided to court the beautiful, young Priscilla Mullins. As was the custom then, he sent a messenger to ask her father, William, if he could call on Priscilla. Standish selected a handsome young man named John Alden to be his messenger. When Priscilla saw John, she made it clear it was *him* she was interested in, not the older Standish. They quickly became engaged and by 1623 were married. Myles eventually married a woman named Barbara, with whom he fathered seven children.

Spring not only brought romance, it also brought some neighbors. On March 16 a scantily clad Wampanoag Indian—one account has him wearing moccasins, a wolf skin around his shoulders, and a smile—strolled into camp and shocked the colonists by greeting them in English, having learned a few words and phrases from Anglo fishermen who passed through the area. His name was Samoset, and he was the first contact they had with any native peoples at Plymouth.

The Wampanoags were a loosely affiliated group of native tribes in Massachusetts and Rhode Island that shared the same language and culture but did not have a centralized ruling body—each tribe was independent.

A week later, on March 22, the colonists had more visitors. The first was Tisquantum, or Squanto, who had spent several years in England and spoke perfect English. He had brought along the Wampanoag chief, Massasoit, and the chief's brother, Quadequina.

In his record of events, Winslow described Massasoit as "a very lusty man, in his best years, an able body, grave of countenance, and spare of speech. In his attire little or nothing differing from the rest of his followers, only in a great chain of white bone beads about his neck . . . at his neck hangs a little bag of tobacco, which he drank and gave us to drink; his face was painted with a sad red like murry, and oiled both head and face, that he looked greasily. All his followers likewise, were in their faces, in part or in whole painted, some black, some red, some yellow, and some white, some with crosses, and other antic works; some had skins on them, and some naked, all strong, tall, all men in appearance."[1]

Using Squanto as a translator, the Puritan leaders wasted no time in setting up a trading relationship and laying the groundwork for a preemptive peace treaty. Everyone by this time was all too familiar with the Lost Colony. They knew it was important coexist peacefully with the native peoples if Plymouth was going to survive and prosper.

Squanto became a trusted member of the colony and was instrumental in helping the Puritan leaders negotiate peace pacts with the area's other tribes. It eventually became clear that Squanto was running some scams for personal gain, such as accepting payment for trying to influence the colonists on behalf of a particular chief or tribe.

For Massasoit and the other Indians, such treachery was a grave offense, and Squanto was sentenced to death. The chief demanded the Puritans turn Squanto over for execution, but Bradford stalled for so long, Massasoit didn't force the issue.

Squanto wasn't the only one grateful for the turn of events. After a year of hardship and suffering, the colonists finally had something to celebrate as they prepared for their first harvest.

The Law Against Christmas

For as devout as the Puritans were, it seems incongruous that they would not celebrate Christmas. However, the Puritans took the Bible literally, and nowhere in the Bible does it say that Christmas would be a holiday.

They were so determined to "purify" their religion from Catholic traditions that in 1659, a law would be passed that made it illegal to celebrate Christmas in Massachusetts.

Thomas F. Reilly

For preventing disorders, arising in several places within this jurisdiction by reason of some still observing such festivals as were superstitiously kept in other communities, to the great dishonor of God and offense of others: it is therefore ordered . . . that whosoever shall be found observing any such day as Christmas or the like, either by forbearing of labor, feasting, or any other way, upon any such account as aforesaid, every such person so offending shall pay . . . a fine to the county.[2]

Although the law was technically repealed in 1681, all children in Massachusetts, regardless of religious affiliation, were required to attend school on Christmas up until 1856. Dating from Puritan times, this and other restrictive laws—such as those against sweeping, cutting hair, and traveling on Sundays—are called blue laws. Their original intent was to protect the sanctity of Sundays by requiring everyone to go to church and meditate on their spiritual life. Over time the lawmakers tried to dictate morality, such as by forbidding the sale of liquor on Sundays—a ban that was overturned in Massachusetts only in 1994.

Many of these Puritanical laws remain on the books, including one that ignited a controversy in 2005. When Whole Foods announced their grocery stores would be open on Thanksgiving, Attorney General Thomas F. Reilly threatened the retailers with criminal prosecution because of the blue laws.

Peter Drummey, librarian at the Massachusetts Historical Society, observed that the Puritans "were less concerned about individual rights than they were about community rights. They were trying to build an ideal community here. And like all Utopian visions, they went too far."[3]

FYI For Your Information

The Puritans continued living on the Mayflower for several months after landing at Plymouth. During that time, the men worked clearing the land and building storehouses and homes. The women stayed on the ship. Fewer than half the Puritans survived the first winter.

Chapter

Settling In Permanently

For generations, the Wampanoag Indians had lived off the land, skillfully adapting their hunting, fishing, and farming to be in sync with nature's yearly cycles. They moved to the cooling shore and fished in spring and summer, then migrated inland and hunted game during the autumn and winter. To the Wampanoags it was intuitive, but the colonists had trouble understanding the pattern. Squanto's help was invaluable. He taught them how to catch eels and showed them which plants were edible and which were poisonous. He also instructed them on the best time of year to plant corn.

As they became more familiar with the natural resources of the area, the Puritans realized that America was truly the land of plenty. In a letter to a friend, Winslow described Plymouth in almost reverential tones:

> I make no question but men might live as contented here
> as in any part of the world. For fish and fowl, we have
> great abundance. . . . Our bay is full of lobsters all the
> summer, and affords a variety of other fish. In September

we can take a hogshead of eels in a night . . . and can dig them out of their beds all the winter. We have mussels . . . at our doors. . . . All the spring-time the earth sends forth naturally very good salad herbs. Here are grapes, white and red, and very sweet and strong also; strawberries, gooseberries, raspberries . . . plums of three sorts, white, black, and red. . . . These things I thought good to let you understand, being the truth of things as near as I could experimentally take knowledge of, and that you might on our behalf give God thanks, who hath dealt so favorably with us.[1]

Resulting from cooperative weather and the tutelage of Squanto, the fall harvest was a much needed and much appreciated bounty. Unlike the previous year, the colonists would have plenty of food to last through the winter. To celebrate, the colony's leaders planned a feast, which took place in October 1621. Contrary to popular thinking, this was not the start of the modern Thanksgiving holiday.

To the Puritans, a day of *Thanksgiving* was a serious day of prayer, and the first one celebrated in Plymouth didn't happen until 1623 when colonists gave thanks for rain after a long drought. What took place in 1621 was more like an English Harvest Home, which was basically a giant picnic party.

Hearing the noise of boisterous settlers shooting off their guns like fireworks, Massasoit showed up with ninety of his men. When he discovered a banquet was being prepared, he sent out some hunters, who brought back five deer. For three days the Wampanoags and the Puritans ate, played games, and relaxed.

The feast would have included waterfowl such as geese or ducks, venison, wild turkeys, lobster, fish, corn, beans, and squash. If pumpkin was served at all, it would have been boiled—not as a dessert in a pie. Fruits and nuts would have also been on the banquet table.

Instead of sitting together for a meal, all the food was put on a serving table, and people ate throughout the day. They'd fill their plate then go sit elsewhere, using a knife and spoon—or more likely their fingers—to eat. The practice of using forks had not yet reached America. The only more formal dining might have been at a head table, where Puritan leaders sat with Massasoit and his top men.

There also weren't any *Pilgrims* at the feast. The word *pilgrim* refers to anyone on a spiritual journey. Twenty years after arriving in Plymouth, Bradford wrote that looking back, the Separatists leaving Leyden "knew they were pilgrims." But even then, he wasn't using the word as a label. According to the Plimoth Plantation website, "Over 150 years later, this quote was taken out of context and

In order to get through the harsh winters, it was important for the Puritans to have enough food. With the help of the American Indians, they learned how to fish, the best crops to plant, and when to plant crops. To celebrate their first successful harvest in 1621, the settlers and their Wampanoag neighbors threw a three-day party that included lobster, eels, fish, venison, and wild turkey.

applied to everyone in Plymouth Colony, including those who were not part of the Leiden [Leyden] congregation Bradford described. The name gained popularity in the 1800s and remains in common usage today."[2]

The term *Pilgrim* came to denote Puritan Separatists in America—those who wanted to create their own church and not just reform the existing Church of England. Just as not all Puritans in England were Separatists, not all Puritans in America were Pilgrims.

A month after the harvest feast, the *Fortune* arrived with thirty-five new colonists, bringing the Plymouth population back up to 85. In the summer of 1623, two more ships, the *Anne* and the *Little James,* dropped off an additional 90 settlers, including family members of existing colonists. With the population of Plymouth now over 170, the community started suffering some growing pains. With more than twice the mouths to feed, there was an ongoing concern over possible food shortages.

The Puritans' most valuable source for growing plentiful crops wasn't there to help them anymore. In November of 1622, while accompanying Bradford on a trading excursion to get some corn seed from the Massachusetts Indians for the coming spring, Squanto became ill.

Knowing he was dying, Squanto asked Bradford to pray for him so that he might go to the heaven of the "Englishmen's God. . . . Squanto continued with them and was their interpreter and was a special instrument sent of God for their good beyond their expectation," Bradford later wrote. He also praised the loyalty Squanto showed the colonists. "He directed them how to set their corn, where to take fish, and to procure other commodities, and was also their pilot to bring them to unknown places for their profit, and never left them till he died."[3]

Indian Technology

The majority of the colonists who came to America felt that they were culturally and technologically superior to the native peoples they encountered. Instead of bustling cities like London, the Indians lived in villages nestled in the untamed wilderness. Their customs—such as wearing little if any clothing in warm weather and painting their faces—seemed primitive and uncivilized to the Europeans.

An Indian village with crops

While the Wampanoags and other tribes may not have made the same medical and scientific advances as seventeenth-century Europeans, the science and technology they did possess made them masters of their environment.

The British literally traveled the world in state-of-the-art vessels that were ideal for sailing the high seas, but they had nothing to get them around the rivers and streams of America. Some of the earliest settlers willingly traded guns and knives for the swift, maneuverable birch-bark canoes the Indians had been making for centuries.

At first, the tribes were very interested in obtaining the colonists' weapons. Once they discovered how long it took to reload a musket and realized they couldn't even see the musket ball when it shot out, most went back to their bow and arrows. A skilled warrior could shoot up to 10 arrows a minute with accuracy up to 200 yards.[4] That, and their knowledge of tracking animals, made them expert hunters.

Perhaps the most important technology developed by Indians was in agriculture. Over thousands of years, indigenous people in the Americas used selective breeding to increase the cob length and size of maize, or corn, until it became the most important crop, yielding significantly more grain per acre than any other cereal.

In addition, Indians used sophisticated farming techniques to increase their harvest. For example, they planted a second crop in between rows of the first crop to preserve the land. They also were the masters of lo-tech. They discovered that burying fish heads alongside the plants acted as a natural fertilizer—although it was a lousy air freshener.

The Massachusetts Bay Colony was founded in 1630 by one thousand Puritans who were led by John Winthrop. Over the next ten years, more settlers poured into Massachusetts than any other colony. Soon, Massachusetts was the most prosperous and most populated colony. To the Puritans' dismay, many of the new settlers arriving in Plymouth, and many young people born in the colonies, did not share their religious zeal.

Chapter

The Puritan Legacy

In 1630, John Winthrop led a group of 1,000 Puritans to found the Massachusetts Bay Colony. Over the next decade, more than 20,000 settlers poured into America, most of them Puritans and most of them joining Winthrop's colony. Alarmed at the number of citizens leaving for Massachusetts, the English government restricted travel, and by 1640, immigration to America had all but stopped.

Even so, the populations of New Plymouth, Virginia, and Massachusetts kept growing and growing. Because people got married fairly young in colonial America and had large families, the population of what would be called New England would double every twenty-eight years. With more people, there were new challenges.

The 103 original New Plymouth colonists all shared a religious and social vision informed by their persecution at the hands of the English Crown and government. However, first-generation Americans had no common threat to bind them and didn't always share in their parents' and grandparent's religious zeal, so strict legal and moral codes were enacted to maintain Puritan ideals within the community.

Nobody was more affected by the influx of settlers than the Wampanoag Indians. While the colonists prospered and their numbers expanded, the indigenous population suffered severe loss of life from diseases introduced by the Europeans. They saw their tribal lands diminishing with each new settlement. Many feared they would lose the homeland they had known for thousands of years.

For fifty-five years, the treaty signed between the original Plymouth colonists and Massasoit was honored, maintaining an often uneasy truce. Each succeeding generation—on both sides—felt less bound by the spirit of peace and cooperation. American-born

The population explosion of Europeans had a disastrous effect on the American Indians. Diseases such as smallpox killed thousands, and colonists appropriated land that belonged for centuries to the tribes. Over time the tensions between local tribes and the settlers grew increasingly hostile, setting the stage for an inevitable showdown.

settlers were greedy for land; younger Indians were determined to save their land and way of life.

Massasoit's youngest son, Metacom, was the leader of the Pokanoket Indians. In 1675, he urged all the Wampanoag tribes to unite in order to drive the Europeans away permanently. He warned colonist Roger Williams of his intent, saying, "I am determined not to live until I have no country."[1]

Metacom was angered by increasingly restrictive treaties, the latest of which prevented him from selling any of his land without colonial approval and ordered his people to turn in all their firearms. The final straw was when three Wampanoags were executed for the murder of another Indian based on the flimsiest of evidence.

The first skirmish took place in June after warriors attacked and burned homes in the village of Swansea. When a settler shot one of the looting Indians, who later died, it ended any hope of a peaceful resolution. Indians retaliated by killing nine colonists, and the war was on.

Having grown up during the peaceful days of the treaty, Metacom was called Philip by the English. The resulting conflict became known as King Philip's War and would be one of the deadliest ever fought on American soil.

Even though there is no evidence that Philip actively led any warriors, he was undoubtedly the inspiration and driving force behind the uprising. In August, Nipmuc Indians joined with Philip's tribe to ambush some colonial troops near Brookfield, just west of Worcester. They killed nine soldiers. The war party chased after the survivors, burning every building they passed along the way. The soldiers and settlers sought refuge in their fort. The Indians then set the fort on fire, leaving those trapped inside with the choice of either staying and burning to death or fleeing to be caught and scalped.

Miraculously, a sudden rainstorm doused the flames, and more soldiers arrived to drive back Philip's forces. Even though the settlers were saved, their town was completely destroyed and would not be resettled for over a decade.

Metacom was the leader of the Pokanoket Indians. Called Philip by the Europeans, he feared his way of life was being destroyed. He was also angry at restrictions being placed on his people, such as having their weapons taken away. Metacom decided to fight and started King Philip's War. Thousands of American Indians— many women and children—were killed in the conflict.

After 71 soldiers were killed in an ambush in the autumn of 1675, many colonists began to consider all Indians the enemy—just because a tribe was peaceful now didn't mean they wouldn't attack tomorrow, they reasoned. The same rationale was behind the Great Swamp Massacre.

In December of that year, General Josiah Winslow, son of Edward Winslow, led a force of 1,000 men from the Plymouth, Massachusetts, and Connecticut colonies into territory held by the Narragansett Indians, who had not joined Philip's call for war. Tipped off by an Indian informant that a large winter camp had been established in a swamp, Winslow attacked. Although the Indians were able to repel the soldiers for a while, they were outmanned and eventually overrun. More than 500 Indians, most of them women and children, were killed—many were burned alive when their wigwams were set on fire.

Outraged by the unprovoked attack, the Narragansett Indians did join with Philip and became among the most ferocious of warriors in their quest for revenge. Town after town was burned. Colonist Mary Rowlandson lived in the town of Lancaster and would later write about her experiences during King Philip's War in the book *The Narrative of the Captivity and the Restoration of Mrs. Mary Rowlandson.*

"At length they came and beset our own house [which served as the garrison], and quickly it was the dolefullest day that ever mine eyes saw. The house stood upon the edge of a hill. Some of the Indians got behind the hill, others into the barn, and others behind anything that would shelter them, from all which places they shot against the house, so that the bullets seemed to fly like hail."[2]

Rowlandson was taken prisoner and eventually ransomed for supplies. Despite the carnage—a greater percentage of the population died in that conflict than any other in American history—Philip simply couldn't match up to the colonists in terms of manpower or provisions. Out of food, their supply of gunpowder nearly depleted, and outnumbered by colonists, Philip never came close to attacking his primary target—Boston.

Slowly the momentum shifted and the Indian warriors were on the run. In May, a young boy who had escaped captivity revealed the location of Philip's main war camp. It was situated near a waterfall so that the Indians could catch fish. In May 1676, Captain William Turner and Captain Samuel Holyoke surprise-attacked Philip's camp. Many of those warriors not shot to death were swept over the falls when they tried to swim to safety. Most of the Indians who escaped fled north. Philip and a small band of loyal warriors stayed, determined to go down fighting.

The end came in the summer of 1676. After Philip had executed one of his own men for suggesting they surrender, a relative of the slain warrior offered to lead the English to Philip's camp. On the morning of August 12, Philip was shot through the heart by an Indian working with colonist Benjamin Church. Philip's War was officially over.

Intending to send a message to any other natives who might consider an uprising, Philip's body was decapitated and cut into four pieces. His head was displayed on a pole in Plymouth for the next 20 years.

It is estimated that 25 percent of the area's Indian population was killed during the war. Many of the survivors were sold into slavery in the Caribbean, including Philip's wife and son. Other Indians were made servants to colonials. It was also made permissible to shoot Indians on sight—the days of treating the natives with equal justice were over.

The destruction of the local tribes opened the door for even greater settlement, and Boston became arguably the most populous and wealthiest city in America. All the individual colonies began exerting more independence from the British Crown. James II was concerned he was losing control and was especially concerned that the colonies were establishing their own armies. In 1686, he ordered that the Plymouth, Rhode Island, Connecticut, and Massachusetts

King James II was worried the colonies were growing too powerful. He was also concerned at how many people were leaving Britain for the New World. James' attempt to replace colonial leaders with British officials failed and helped fan the colonies' growing spirit of independence.

Bay colonies be merged into the Dominion of New England. He also replaced elected leaders with handpicked officials.

The Dominion was dissolved three years later, after James was overthrown. In 1691 the new joint rulers, Mary II and William of Orange, ordered that Plymouth be annexed to Massachusetts, ending its individual history—and signaling the end of Puritan domination. The next year brought the hysteria of the Salem witch trials. Accused of being witches, nineteen innocent people were burned and dozens more were imprisoned. After that, the Puritans' image never recovered.

Massachusetts passed a law prohibiting Puritans from discriminating against Quakers and Anglicans, which greatly undermined the Puritans' political power. By the beginning of the eighteenth century, as the colony became more diverse, the Puritans' days of influence and leadership were over.

Still, their legacy remains. Priscilla Mullins's descendants include President John Adams, poets Henry Wadsworth Longfellow and William Cullen Bryant, Vice President Dan Quayle, Orson Welles, and even Marilyn Monroe.

Other historic American figures such as Presidents Franklin D. Roosevelt and George W. Bush, Humphrey Bogart, Mormon Church founder Joseph Smith, and poet Ralph Waldo Emerson can trace their bloodlines directly to Elizabeth Tilley.

Not only did the Puritans indelibly affect modern America through the traditional values that have been passed down through the generations, but they still reside within the very blood of many American citizens.

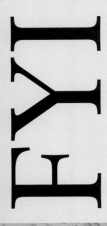
FYI

Crime and Punishment

The first laws adopted by the Puritan leaders at Plymouth Colony were simple and dealt primarily with trade, hunting, housing, and land issues such as ordinances against cutting down trees without permission. There were also restrictions on craftsmen from doing work for any "foreigners" if the colony needed their expertise.

The Book of the General Laws of the Inhabitants of the Jurisdiction of New-Plimouth, 1685

As the population grew, so did the need for a formal court system. In 1636 the Colony of New Plymouth established the first formal legal code in North America. Detailed, wide-ranging, and covering both criminal and civil matters, the code also contained a basic guarantee of individual rights, such as a guarantee of trial by jury. It also reaffirmed that no law could be enacted without the consent of the colony's freemen.

The code specified five capital crimes, or offenses that could bring the death penalty. They were willful murder, adultery, arson of ships or houses, entering into a compact with the devil through witchcraft, and various sexual crimes.

Although anyone caught committing adultery could be put to death, that sentence was never imposed. Instead, cheating spouses were subjected to pubic whippings and were forced to wear an *A*—the mark of an adulterer—on their clothing.

The first person executed for murder was *Mayflower* passenger John Billington. Capital punishment was carried out by hanging. Nor were women immune. In 1648, Alice Bishop was executed for stabbing her four-year-old daughter while the child slept.

The 1636 code criminalized only social conduct. However, when the code was revised in 1685, laws were added intended to control both personal morality and religious conduct. It merged religious beliefs and civil responsibility into a kind of theocracy—a government based on a specific religious belief.

It is more than a little ironic that the Puritans had come full circle: from being a group of people who left their homeland in pursuit of religious freedom from those in authority, to being the authority trying to legally force *their* religious beliefs onto all other citizens. Ultimately that intolerance would prove their undoing.

Chapter Notes

Chapter One
The Lost Colony

1. Willie Drye, "America's Lost Colony: Can New Dig Solve Mystery?" *National Geographic News,* March 2, 2004, http://news.nationalgeographic.com/news/2004/03/0302_040302_lostcolony.html

2. Ralph Lane, "The Colony At Roanoke [1586]," http://www.national-center.org/ColonyofRoanoke.html

Chapter Two
Persecution

1. Caleb Johnson, "Cross-Sections of the *Mayflower,*" MayflowerHistory.com, http://www.mayflowerhistory.com/History/mflower5.php

2. 4literature.net, *Bradford and Winslow's Journal by William Bradford,* http://www.4literature.net/William_Bradford/Bradford_s_and_Winslow_s_Journal/4.html

3. Plimoth Plantation, *Sewing in Plymouth Colony,* http://www.plimoth.org/learn/history/colony/sewing.asp

Chapter Three
A Deadly Winter

1. Winslow, Edward, "A Relation or Journal of the Proceedings of the Plantation Settled at Plymouth," *Mourt's Relation: A Journal of the Pilgrims at Plymouth,* Dwight B. Heath, editor (New York: Corinth Books, 1963); The Plymouth Colony Archive Project, http://etext.lib.virginia.edu/users/deetz/Plymouth/mourt1.html *(Author's note: Some Native Americans boiled or chewed tobacco leaves, then drank the juice to counteract mild illnesses, colds, or chills, and as a cure for snakebites.)*

2. Mac Daniel, "Largely Ignored, Puritan Laws Like 'Common Day of Rest' Revisited for the Holidays," *Boston Globe,* December 4, 2005, http://www.boston.com/news/local/massachusetts/articles/2005/12/04/back_and_blue

3. Ibid.

Chapter Four
Settling In Permanently

1. Edward Winslow, "A Letter Sent from New England to a Friend in These Parts," *Mourt's Relation: A Journal of the Pilgrims at Plymouth,* Ed. Dwight B. Heath (New York: Corinth Books, 1963); The Plymouth Colony Archive Project, http://etext.lib.virginia.edu/users/deetz/Plymouth/mourt6.html

2. Plimoth Plantation.com, *1627 Pilgrim Village,* http://www.plimoth.org/visit/what/1627.asp

3. William Bradford, [1650] *Of Plymouth Plantation, 1620–1647.* Samuel Eliot Morison, ed. (New York: Knopf, 1852).

4. Charles C. Mann, "Native Ingenuity," *The Boston Globe,* September 4, 2005, http://www.boston.com/news/globe/ideas/articles/2005/09/04/native_ingenuity/?page=full

Chapter Five
The Puritan Legacy

1. Michael Tougias, "Revisiting King Philip's War," *Boston Globe,* January 28, 2001.

2. Mary Rowlandson, *The Narrative of the Captivity and the Restoration of Mrs. Mary Rowlandson, 1682,* http://www.library.csi.cuny.edu/dept/history/lavender/rownarr.html

Chronology

1603	Sir Walter Raleigh is convicted of conspiring to have James I removed from the throne.
1607	Large groups of Puritans begin immigrating to Leyden in the Netherlands, seeking religious freedom.
1619	Puritans receive land charter to establish colony in Virginia.
1620	Unable to sail to Virginia, the *Mayflower* arrives at Provincetown on November 11; the Mayflower Compact is drafted.
1621	In spring, Samoset greets the settlers. William Bradford is named governor. The first Thanksgiving is celebrated in October.
1622	Squanto, who has been invaluable to the settlers, dies.
1623	The *Anne* and *Little James* bring 90 more colonists in July and August; John Alden and Priscilla Mullins marry.
1636	New Plymouth establishes the first formal legal code in the colonies.
1648	Alice Bishop becomes the first woman executed in the colonies.
1659	To "purify" their religion from Catholic traditions, Puritans in Massachusetts make it illegal to celebrate Christmas.
1675	King Philip's War begins.
1676	King Philip is shot in August, and his war ends. Governor Josiah Winslow approves the sale of Native Americans as slaves.
1685	The penal code is amended to cover religious conduct.
1686	James II merges New Plymouth, Rhode Island, Connecticut, and Massachusetts Bay colonies into Dominion of New England.
1689	Dominion of New England is dissolved after James II is overthrown.
1691	Plymouth is annexed to Massachusetts and ceases being a separate colony.

Timeline in History

1564	Shakespeare is born.
1577	Sir Francis Drake sails around the world.
1582	Gregorian calendar is introduced.
1587	Mary, Queen of Scots, is executed.
1592	Remains of Pompeii are discovered.
1603	James I becomes King of England.
1607	French settlers found Quebec.
1610	Tea is introduced to England.
1611	The King James Version of the Bible is published.
1616	Smallpox epidemic decimates New England Native Americans.
1619	Slaves are first brought to Jamestown.
1623	Baghdad is conquered by the Persians.
1626	Dutch colonist Peter Minuit buys Manhattan Island from Native Americans for 60 guilders—or about $24.
1633	Galileo is put on trial for heresy.
1636	Harvard University is founded.
1637	At Mystic Massacre in Connecticut, over 400 Pequots, mostly women and children, are killed.
1640	*The Bay Psalm Book* is the first book printed in Colonial America.
1653	Taj Mahal is completed.
1656	Quakers arrive in Boston from England.
1660	The Dutch settle South Africa.
1665	The plague kills up to 60,000 Londoners.
1667	John Milton writes *Paradise Lost*.
1670	Pocket watches add minute hands.
1689	Peter the Great becomes czar of Russia.
1692	The Salem witch trials begin in Massachusetts.

Further Reading

For Young Adults

Fritz, Jean. *The Lost Colony of Roanoke.* New York: Putnam Juvenile, 2004.

Harness, Cheryl. *The Adventurous Life of Myles Standish and the Amazing-but-True Survival Story of Plymouth Colony.* Washington, DC: National Geographic Children's Books, 2006.

Rice, Earle, Jr. *The Life and Times of Sir Walter Raleigh.* Hockessin, DE: Mitchell Lane Publishers, 2007.

Roop, Connie and Peter. *Pilgrim Voices: Our First Year in the New World.* New York: Walker and Company, 1997.

Works Consulted

Bradford, William. [1650] *Of Plymouth Plantation, 1620–1647.* Samuel Eliot Morison, ed. New York: Knopf, 1852.

Daniel, Mac. "Largely Ignored, Puritan Laws Like 'Common Day of Rest' Revisited for the Holidays," *Boston Globe,* December 4, 2005, http://www.boston.com/news/local/articles/2005/12/04/back_and_blue/

Fennell, Christopher. *Plymouth Colony Legal Structure.* Seminar Paper, UVA Anth 509, Spring 1998.

Langdon, George D. *Pilgrim Colony: A History of New Plymouth 1620–1691.* New Haven: Yale University Press, 1966.

Mann, Charles C. "Native Ingenuity," *The Boston Globe,* September 4, 2005, http://www.boston.com/news/globe/ideas/articles/2005/09/04/native_ingenuity/?page=full

Stratton, Eugene Aubrey. *Plymouth Colony: Its History & People 1620–1691.* Salt Lake City: Ancestry Publishing, 1986.

Tougias, Michael. "Revisiting King Philip's War," *Boston Globe,* January 28, 2001.

Tusser, Thomas. *500 Points of Good Husbandrie.* W. Payne, ed. London: English Dialect Society, 1878.

Winslow, Edward. "A Letter Sent from New England," *Mourt's Relation: A Journal of the Pilgrims at Plymouth.* Dwight B. Heath, ed. New York: Corinth Books, 1963.

The Plymouth Colony Archive Project, http://etext.lib.virginia.edu/users/deetz/Plymouth/mourt6.html

Goldstein, Karin. "Sewing in Plymouth Colony," http://www.plimoth.org/learn/history/colony/sewing.asp

MayflowerHistory.com, http://www.mayflowerhistory.com/index.php

Plimoth Plantation, http://www.plimoth.org/learn/history/colony/index.asp

The Plymouth Colony Archive Project, http://etext.lib.virginia.edu/users/deetz

Sail 1620, http://sail1620.org/discover.shtml

Waldon, R. "Pilgrim History," http://www.richmondancestry.org/pilgrim.shtml

On the Internet

Plimoth Plantation
http://www.plimoth.org

The Plymouth Colony Archive Project
http://etext.lib.virginia.edu/users/deetz/

Glossary

Anglicans
(ANG-luh-kens)
People who follow the teachings of the traditional Church of England.

annex
(AA-neks)
To make part of something larger.

annul
(uh-NUL)
To declare invalid.

armada
(ar-MAH-duh)
A large fleet of warships.

charter
(CHAR-tur)
A legal document granting the right to use a specified parcel of land.

currency
(KUR-en-see)
Any form of money in public use.

fleur-de-lis
(FLUR-duh-lee)
A flowerlike design that was the unofficial symbol of France from the fifteenth to the early nineteenth century.

freeman
(FREE-man)
A citizen of the colony; only adult males could be freemen.

musket
(MUS-kit)
A shoulder gun loaded through the muzzle used from the late sixteenth through the eighteenth century.

pilgrim
(PIL-grim)
A person who travels to a foreign land, often on a religious journey.

preemptive
(pree-EMP-tiv)
To prevent or alter an event before it happens.

Puritans
(PYOOR-uh-tins)
Protestants who wanted to purify the Anglican Church of Catholic influences.

Separatists
(SEP-rah-tists)
Radical Protestants who wanted to separate from the Church of England rather than reform it.

smallpox
(SMALL-poks)
A highly contagious disease that causes painful blisters and in colonial times was often fatal.

Wampanoag
(WOM-pah-nog)
A group of American Indians who lived in Massachusetts and Rhode Island when the Puritans arrived in America.

weroance
(WAYR-oh-ens)
A tribal leader in the Chesapeake Bay area.

Index